DARK SKY DANCING

The four seasons in haiku

RICHARD STEWART

Artwork: Anne-Marie Stewart

Some of the haiku in this collection have been published previously in the following: *Butterfly Days, Cycling World, Dial 174, Earth Love, Green Man, Haiku Scotland*, Newsletters of Butterfly Conservation Branches: *Cambridge and Essex, Devon, Dorset, Kent, Lincolnshire and Upper Thames, Phoenix New Life Poetry, Poetry Cornwall, Poetry Monthly, Quantum Leap, Remembrance, Suffolk and Norfolk Life*.

Thanks go to Robert Kensit and Jean Saunders
for all their help in producing this book.

Cover illustration: *Colours Changing Hue* by Anne-Marie Stewart

Introduction

Each of these four sections has twenty eight haiku, covering the seasons of the year and roughly following the day from dawn and early morning to dusk and night. The vast majority are wedded to the natural cycle of the year. A few, deliberately and conversely, comment on that other more urban world, often divorced from nature. I am aware of all the current arguments in favour of a more flexible style of haiku but have chosen to make each one in this selection fit the traditional format of three lines and seventeen syllables, five, seven and five respectively. Each haiku has a title, since I believe it gives them more of a separate identity. The art quilt illustrations are by my wife, Anne-Marie Stewart. Bearing in mind the length of haiku, it is appropriate to make this a short introduction.

Richard Stewart, 2010.

Autumn

Bawdsey Cliffs

Early

First train of the day
And across grey silent fields
Feeding rooks take flight.

Dawn

Into a rich world
With everywhere the glitter
Of pearl necklaces.

Branch

A bright autumn flame
Rekindled every morning
By the sun's warm rays.

Cattawade

How the landscape glows
With these two farmyard buildings
And their bright red roofs.

Seller

It's the magazine
That makes me invisible
This new Big Issue.

From Paddington

Within six minutes
Mobile call ipod laptop
Personal windows.

Landfill

Centuries from now
Recyclers will label us
The plastic bag age.

Composition

One pyracantha
Orange berries in the sun
And a blue ladder.

Late September

On a cold grey day
Praise helianthus flowers
Each a golden sun.

October

Flame red and scarlet
The creeper's leaves blaze behind
A black fire escape.

Coast

Deep in the dark pines
Flashes of sunshine reveal
Migrating goldcrests.

Banquet

For the autumn wasps
On sunlit ivy flowers
A requiem feast.

Blessing

This fruiting ivy
Flickers with sudden dark fire
A red admiral.

Woodcock

Sun glints on an eye
Slowly traces the still bird
Bedded in dry leaves.

Transformation

From a coal blackness
To this large eyed radiance
Peacock's open wings.

Taste

Along the main road
Restless with speeding traffic
Unpicked blackberries.

Brambles

Two feeding commas
On fermenting blackberries
Out of the wind's edge.

Snug

Dines on apple cores
Carrots and soft bananas
Vole in the compost.

Fall

Under the brown trees
In a cold autumn back yard
Warm orange carpets.

Benacre: 1

Two men climb this cliff
Ignoring signs while below
A hungry sea waits.

Benacre: 2

Shots come from the wood
And across the rainswept broad
Rafts of gulls weave white.

Treecreeper

A slender scratching
Of sharp claws and probing eye
Searching each fissure.

Above

Of those going home
How many looked up to see
A sudden rainbow?

Expectant

Near the restaurant
Along a thin strip of grass
Two hungry foxes.

Reversion

Clod becomes creature
As a still hare starts to move
Welcoming the night.

Remote

Out in the darkness
Far from the bright comfort zone
A hunting owl screams.

Release

Man in a smart suit
Ending the long working day
Tears off his black tie.

Driver

His hands on the wheel
And within their warm embrace
Forty precious lives.

Winter

Four of Harts

Bedroom Window

Opens to darkness
And restless unseen blackbirds
Singing for the light.

Transformed

Early morning sun
Catches these high flying gulls
Turns them into gold.

Waxwings

They have stripped the trees
Just a few berries remain
Each a parting gift.

Garden

This sudden rainbow
On the sunlit balls of fat
As a starling feeds.

Bustle

It's commuter time
Business jabber and jostling
Nowhere to be still.

Solstice

Grey sky but the sun
Covers these cold bare cobbles
With yellow flowers.

Storm

Throughout the long day
Water gushes from a pipe
And Africa weeps.

Delivery

From the cloak of rain
A quick flash of bright orange
As the paper comes.

Lark's Meadow

Yes there were larks here
Hence the name for these houses
Bricked into bare soil.

Passing Train

Lapwings rise as one
Playing games of chequerboard
Against a grey sky.

Visitor

Has become a guest
Uninvited through our sleep
This sudden snowfall.

Nocturnal

The night wanderers
Leave tracks threaded with stitches
In a quilt of snow.

Cotoneaster

Wind driven deep snow
Forces the tall berried boughs
Back to their deep roots.

Tits

Blown across the lawn
To feed on snow caked fat balls
Little scraps of life.

Benison

Deep comfort of snow
The way it hushes each sound
And covers all scars.

Frost

The path underfoot
Crunches and snaps while below
Badgers are sleeping.

Endurance

Blackbirds on the grass
Warmed by late evening sunshine
Before their long roost.

Migrants

Beyond the sunset
Dark against deep drifts of snow
Hungry redwings feed.

Town Roost

Above the mobiles
In silent murmurations
Shoals of starlings dance.

Late January

Melting ice on grass
Reflects the full moon's passage
Through layers of cloud.

Revealed

See how the moonlight
On a wall's encrusted moss
Sets the frost sparkling.

Evening Match

Before the floodlights
Hunting owl is motionless
Golden as a god.

Outside

Huddling together
In the freezing winter night
Listening to foxes.

Searching

Cutting the blackness
Sharper than any traffic
Barking fox on heat.

Gloaming

Most lonely of all
An owl's cry echoing through
The gathering dark.

Midnight

On this long clear night
Full moon and sharp frost create
A world of silver.

February

Beneath a blanket
Of soft snow on deep ivy
Yellow brimstones wait.

March

Cold earth is turning
Slip sliding into the spring
As icicles melt.

Spring

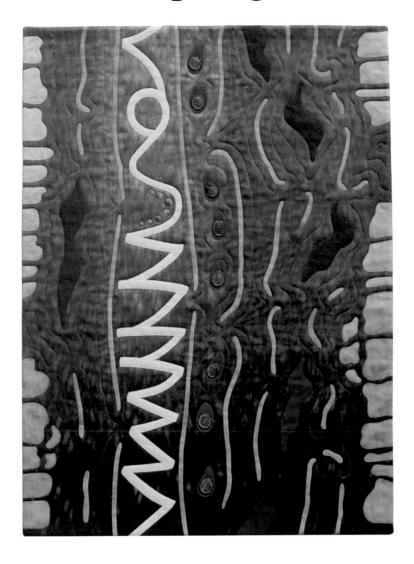

Life Unravelling

Survivors

Sunlight on hard frost
And deep within a green pine
Red admirals stir.

Daffodils

An army is here
With spears and yellow trumpets
Heralding the spring.

Warbler

Near the main station
In early morning silence
A blackcap singing.

Reaction

Now spring has arrived
With the loud insistent song
Of hungry chainsaws.

Morning

Rain and cloud conspire
Drawing colour from the day
Then the white gulls come.

Charm

Tinkling from above
The way zephyrs stir wind bells
As goldfinches pass.

Contrast

Yellow alyssum
Has flowered just in time for
The passing blackbird.

Dispersal

Smoke above mown grass
As the pine's golden candles
Are stirred in a breeze.

April

Just five red tulips
Full flowering tall and proud
Against a dark bush.

Gardening

They are closer now
Their soft calls surrounding her
Long tailed tits feeding.

Unseen

In the grey covert
High above concealed fox traps
A nightingale sings.

Wood pigeon

Deep contented call
From within the conifers
Sitting on her nest.

Question

Fourteen magpies fly
Chattering to the tall trees
Spring blessing or curse?

Fishing

Sun on a heron
Turning its hunched grey into
An old jagged post.

Butterflies

Two peacocks fly up
Spiralling in a bright sky
Covered by larksong.

Larvae

The green consumers
Voyagers through inner space
Instar to instar.

Chilford Hall

Trees rot and crumble
Fall in storms or bow to saws
But the rooks remain.

Confluence

Saturday morning
Stills to the soothing fingers
Of a street harpist.

Armed

Boy and bubble gun
Out to shoot the big bad world
With rings of rainbows.

Aware

Mad hare lolloping
Down the middle of a lane
Hedges on both sides.

Courtship

A storm is coming
But marsh harriers pursue
Their dark sky dancing.

Swallows

How they sip water
As if bestowing on it
Some kind of blessing.

Evening

April robin sings
His throbbing breast deeper red
As the sun goes down.

Survival

Prefers hedge garlic
Warmed by rays of evening sun
Roosting orange tip.

Passengers

Deep in newspapers
Nodding to a plugged in beat
Missing the sunset.

Dusk

As day softly fades
And dog walkers have gone home
The badgers emerge.

Return

Too dark to see deer
Are shadows within shadows
Possessing the night.

Late

The path of a snail
On the grey lamplit pavement
Silvering this night.

Summer

Set the Controls for the Heart of the Sun

Curious

Watching trains passing
Close to the main London line
Early morning fox.

Airport

Sunlight on parked cars
Shoals of jellyfish stranded
On a concrete beach.

Awayday

Go on spoil yourself
Spend a day somewhere remote
Without a mobile.

Flag

Around a dark edge
Of the deeply silted pond
Yellow iris blooms.

Memory

Frothing meadowsweet
Flowering tall by the path
Fragrance of childhood.

Caught

On the tall grass heaps
Bright cut wings of tiger moths
Discarded jewels.

Large White

Cabbage destroyer
But against a deep blue sky
Admire its beauty.

Emergence

Over a small pond
Coupled azure damselflies
Smoke on the water.

Summer Snow

Snowfall in late June
Soft whiteness across the path
As a poplar blooms.

Speckled Woods

Two brown butterflies
Dancing beneath dappled leaves
Battling for sunspots.

Unexpected

The heat of the day
Brings to our small water bowl
A stumbling hedgehog.

Testing

Young jays on the lawn
Exploring all food prospects
Hunger will teach them.

Trafalgar Square

Climate change rally
And above Nelson's column
Mocking vapour trails.

Accustomed

The smart town pigeons
Next to the recycling bin
Don't stir a feather.

Calm

See the tall green trees
How they link this earth and sky
Offer us deep peace.

Wheatfen Broad

At the woodland edge
Where sun spangles into shade
A tall white foxglove.

Drought

This too is summer
The long deep pond contracted
Fish gasping for life.

Birthday

Soft rain in dry dunes
A slow unfurling of snails
Just the two of us.

Shower

And after the rain
Has ended its soft blessing
Everything so green.

Still

Along the leaf spine
Brimstone caterpillar rests
Green on green unseen.

Painted Ladies

Resisting nectar
They head inland on fast wings
Millions of migrants.

Grass Snake

Caught in fruit netting
Just a flicker of its tongue
Signals the life force.

Scarlet

At the building site
Consuming a spent soil pile
Fire of red poppies.

Park

Loud group on the stage
And in a nearby green oak
Purple hairstreaks dance.

Late Summer

On top of soft plum
The feeding red admiral
A deep crimson slash.

Silent

High above the roar
Of speeding homeward traffic
Grey heron passes.

Aerial

Does a sleeping swift
Dark against the blue of night
Have deep dreams of earth?

Buddleia

Through the night's stillness
Ghost moths on hovering wings
Hunt the perfumed dark.